Selections from the "Book of Songs"

Translated by Yang Xianyi, Gladys Yang and Hu Shiguang

Panda Books

Panda Books

First edition, 1983

Copyright 1983 by CHINESE LITERATURE

ISBN 0-8351-1080-x

Published by CHINESE LITERATURE, Beijing (37), China

Distributed by China Publications Centre (GUOJI SHUDIAN)
P.O. Box 399, Beijing, China

Printed in the People's Republic of China

CONTENTS

Crying Ospreys

MERRILY the ospreys cry,
On the islet in the stream.
Gentle and graceful is the girl,
A fit wife for the gentleman.

Short and long the floating water plants,
Left and right you may pluck them.
Gentle and graceful is the girl,
Awake he longs for her and in his dreams.

When the courtship has failed,
Awake he thinks of her and in his dreams.
Filled with sorrowful thoughts,
He tosses about unable to sleep.

Short and long the floating water plants,

Left and right you may gather them.

Gentle and graceful is the girl,

He'd like to wed her, the *qin* and *se** playing.

Short and long the floating water plants,

Left and right you may collect them.

Gentle and graceful is the girl,

He'd like to marry her, bells and drums beating.

---

* Two traditional Chinese musical instruments, rather like the zither; the former has seven strings and the latter twenty-five strings.

The Peach Tree Is Slender and Sturdy

THE peach tree is slender and sturdy,
Flaming red are its blossoms.
The girl is getting married,
Most suitable for the house.

The peach tree is slender and sturdy,
Luscious and abundant is its fruit.
The girl is getting married,
Most suitable for the home.

The peach tree is slender and sturdy,
Exuberant and green are its leaves.
The girl is getting married,
Most suitable for the family.

Gathering Plantain

GATHERING plantain,
Here we go plucking it;
Gathering plantain,
Here we go picking it.

Gathering plantain,
Quick fingers strip it;
Gathering plantain,
By handfuls pull it.

Gathering plantain,
Here we fill skirts with it;
Gathering plantain,
Belt up full skirts!

In the South There Is a High Tree

IN the south there is a high tree;
It gives no shelter.
Beyond the Han roams a maid;
I cannot reach her.
Ah, the Han it is so wide
I cannot swim it,
And the Yangzi is so long
I cannot pass it!

From the tangled undergrowth
I shall cut the thistles.
When the maid comes to marry me,
I shall feed her horses.
Ah, the Han it is so wide

I cannot swim it,
And the Yangzi is so long
I cannot pass it!

From the tangled undergrowth
I shall cut the wormwood.
When the maid comes to marry me,
I shall feed her ponies.
Ah, the Han it is so wide
I cannot swim it,
And the Yangzi is so long
I cannot pass it!

The Paths Are Drenched with Dew

THE paths are drenched with dew,

Yet we must leave before dawn.

Why should I fear to walk through heavy dew?

Who says that the sparrow has no beak?

How else could it pierce my roof?

Who says that my daughter is unwed?

Why should you send me to jail?

But though you send me to jail,

You cannot add her to your family.

Who says that the rat has no teeth?
How else could it pierce my wall?
Who says that my daughter is unwed?

Why should you take me to court?
But though you take me to court,
I shall still refuse your demand.

Plop, Fall the Plums

PLOP, fall the plums;
Of ten on the tree, seven remain;
Let those who would court me
Come before the lucky day slips by.

Plop, fall the plums;
Of ten on the tree, three remain;
For those who would court me
Now is the time!

Plop, fall the plums;
Place them in flat baskets;
Let those who would court me
Come to the gathering!*

---

* It was a Zhou Dynasty custom to hold a gathering in mid-
spring when unmarried men of thirty and unmarried girls of twenty
would pair off, dispensing with the usual marriage ceremony.

The Roebuck

IN the wilds there lies a dead roebuck
Covered over with white rushes;
A girl is longing for love,
A fine fellow tempts her.

In the woods are bushes,
And in the wilds a dead deer
Bound with white rushes.
The girl is fair as jade.

"Oh, soft now and gently;
Don't touch my sash!
Take care, or the dog will bark!"

The Boat of Cypress Wood

FREELY floats the boat of cypress wood,
Tossing about along the stream.
Eyes open, I can't fall asleep,
As if my heart were heavy with grief.
It's not that I've no wine to drink,
Or nowhere to enjoy visiting.

My heart's not like a bronze mirror,
Absorbing the reflection of everything.
I've brothers, elder and younger,
But not one is trustworthy.
When I tried to pour out my grievances,
I found them furious with me.

My heart's not like a stone,
It can't be turned and moved easily.

My heart's not like a mat,
It can't be rolled up at will.
With dignity and honour,
I'll never flinch or yield.

My heart's weighed down with vexation,
Against me the villains bear a grudge.
Excessive distress I've been confronted with,
Too much indignity I've been treated with.
Meditating silently on this,
I beat my breast when the sad truth dawns upon
    me.

Oh sun, oh moon,
Why are you always so dim?
My heart stained with sorrow,
Cannot be washed clean like dirty clothes.
I reflect silently on this,
And cannot spread my wings and soar high.

Swallows

SWALLOWS winging their flight,
Short and long are their feathers.
Homewards the lady is going,
Far beyond the fields I see her off.
Gazing till she is out of sight,
My tears fall like rain.

Swallows winging their flight,
Up and down they hover.
Homewards the lady is going,
Far away I see her off.
Gazing till she is out of sight,
I stand a long time weeping.

Swallows winging their flight,
High and low is their song.
Homewards the lady is going,
Far to the south I see her off.
Gazing till she is out of sight,
My heart is filled with sorrow.

Faithful is this lady Zhong,
Her heart honest and deep.
Gentle and kind-hearted,
She remains careful and virtuous.
With her fond memories of the late duke,
She's always consoled and encouraged me.

t's Near Dusk

IT'S near dusk,
It's near dusk,
Why not go home?
If not for the sake of the lord's corvée,
Why should we suffer the heavy dew?

It's near dusk,
It's near dusk,
Why not go home?
If not for the sake of the lord's person,
Why should we toil in the mire?

The Quiet Girl

A quiet girl and lovely
Was to meet me at the turret by the wall;
But she is nowhere to be seen,
And I scratch my head, perplexed.

A quiet girl and pretty
Gives me a blade of red grass;
A splendid blade of red grass —
I take pleasure in its beauty.

From the meadows she brings me a shoot,
Beautiful and rare;
It is not the shoot that is lovely,
But it was given me by a lovely girl.

Dazzling the New Tower

DAZZLING the new tower
By the brimming river.
In place of the good match sought,
A loathsome toad.

Lofty the new tower
By the smooth-flowing river.
In place of the good match sought,
A stinking toad.

A net set for fish
Caught a paddock.
In place of the good match sought,
An ugly hunchback.

This song satirizes Duke Xuan of Wei, who took his son's bride
as his own wife, and to welcome her built a tower by the Yellow
River.

Hoping to Live with Her Lord Till Death

HOPING to live with her lord till death,

She wears a coronet with six jewels.

It looks so stately and graceful,

Like imposing mountains and elegant rivers.

The painted garment fits her well.

But fate has been bad to her,

What unavoidable misfortune!

So bright and gorgeous

Are the pheasant feathers painted on her gown.

Jet-black hair crowns her head like clouds,

No false locks does she need.

Her eardrops are made of jade,

Her head scratcher of ivory.

Broad is her forehead and fair-complexioned.

Why should she go to heaven?

Why present herself before the gods?

So exquisite and resplendent

Is her snow-white ceremonial attire.

Over fine crêpe underclothing

She wears a close-fitting undergarment.

Bright and sparkling are her eyes,

Broad is her brow.

Truly, only a lady like her

Can be a beauty of this state.

The Rat Has a Skin

THE rat has a skin,

Yet a man may lack decency.

A man without decency,

What is he doing, that he does not die?

The rat has teeth,

Yet a man may have no restraint.

A man with no restraint,

What is he waiting for, that he does not die?

The rat has limbs,

Yet a man may have no manners.

A man with no manners

Had best quickly die.

I Ride, I Gallop

I ride, I gallop,

Bearing words of comfort for the lord of Wei,

Spurring my horse on and on

To the city of Cao;*

But the elders too have made the long journey,

And my heart is troubled.

You may oppose me,

But I cannot go back;

My plan is less far-fetched

Than your worthless scheme.

You may oppose me

But you cannot stop me;

---

* After the state of Wei was overthrown by the Di tribesmen in 660 B.C., the defeated took refuge in the city of Cao and set up a new lord of Wei, whose younger sister, Lady Mu, came from the state of Xu with a proposal to ask help from other countries. To her anger, the men of Xu opposed her plan, and sent their councillors to Cao to thwart it.

My plan is better thought out
Than your worthless scheme.

I climb a sloping mound
To gather toad-lilies;
Though a woman is easily moved,
She knows what is right.
The men of Xu blame me —
Overbearing fools!

I walk in the fields;
Thick and green grows the wheat;
We must turn for aid to some mighty state —
Who feels for us will help us.

Councillors and nobles,
The fault lies not with me;
All your hundred schemes
Count for less than what I shall do!

The Buxom Lady

THE buxom lady is big and tall,

Over a brocade garment she wears a cape.

A daughter of the Duke of Qi,

She is now the bride of our Duke of Wei;

Younger sister of the heir to Qi,

Sister-in-law of the Marquis of Xing,

The lord of Tan is her brother-in-law.

Her delicate fingers as tender grass,

Her skin white and smooth as lard,

Her neck long and soft as a longicorn's larva,

Her teeth even and white as melon seeds,

Her head full and square, her brows long and curved,

Sweet smile dimpling the corners of her mouth,

Her pretty eyes, the black and white clearly defined.

The buxom lady is tall and big,

On the outskirts she halts for a rest.

The four steeds vigorous and strong,

The red silk trappings on their bits imposing,

In a pheasant-feathered, curtained carriage she reaches the court.

Leave the court early, high officials,

Don't trouble and tire our duke!

Vast and mighty are the waters of the Yellow River,

Northward its jubilant waves surge;

When a net is played out swishing,

Carp and sturgeon leap and splash.

The reeds by the banks towering high,

All her bridal maids are slender and richly dressed,

All her warriors gallant and impressive.

A Simple Fellow

A simple fellow, all smiles,
Brought cloth to exchange for thread,
Not in truth to buy thread
But to arrange about me.
I saw you across the Qi
As far as Dunqiu;
It was not I who wanted to put it off,
But you did not have a proper match-maker.
I begged you not to be angry
And fixed autumn as the time.

I climbed the city wall
To watch for your return to the pass;

And when you did not come
My tears fell in floods;
Then I saw you come,
And how gaily I laughed and talked!
You consulted tortoise-shell and milfoil,*
And they showed nothing unlucky;
You came with your cart
And took me off with my dowry.

Before the mulberry sheds its leaves,
How green and fresh they are!
Ah, turtle-dove,
Do not eat the mulberries!
Ah, girls,
Do not take your pleasure with men!
A man can take pleasure
And get away with it,
But a girl
Will never get away with it.

---

* Used for divination.

The mulberry sheds its leaves
Yellow and sere;
After going to you
Three years I supped on poverty.
Deep are the waters of the Qi;
They wet the curtains as the carriage crossed,
I did no wrong,
You were the one to blame;
It was you who were faithless
And changed.

Three years I was your wife,
Never idle in your house,
Rising early and retiring late
Day after day.
All went smoothly
Till you turned rough;
And my brothers, not knowing,
Laughed and joked with me as before.

Alone, thinking over my fate,
I could only lament.

I had hoped to grow old with you,
Now the thought of old age grieves my heart.
The Qi has its shores,
The Shi its banks;
How happy we were, our hair in tufts,*
How fondly we talked and laughed,
How solemnly swore to be true!
I must think no more of the past;
The past is done with —
Better let it end like this!

---

* Young people, before coming of age, tied their hair in two
tufts.

Bo Is So Brave

BO is so brave,
A hero in our state!
Grasping his lance
He fights in the king's vanguard.

Since Bo went to the east
My hair has been unkempt as wind-blown thistle.
It is not that I have no hair-oil,
But for whom should I want to beautify myself?

Let it rain, let it rain!
But instead the sun shines bright.
I keep longing for Bo,
Heedless of my aching head.

Where can I find the herb of forgetfulness
To plant behind the house?
I keep longing for Bo,
Though it makes me sick at heart.

Quince

A quince she threw to me,
A jade pendant I gave her in return.
It was not just a requital,
But to show I'd love her for ever.

A peach she threw to me,
A gem pendant I gave her in return.
It was not just a requital,
But to show I'd love her for ever.

A plum she threw to me,
A jasper pendant I gave her in return.
It was not just a requital,
But to show I'd love her for ever.

The Millet Is Dense and Tall

THE millet is dense and tall,

The sorghum is in sprout.

I walk on slowly,

My heart shaken within me.

Those who know me say that my heart is sad;

Those who do not know me ask for what I am
searching.

Oh, grey heaven stretching endlessly away,

Who has done this to me?

The millet is dense and tall,

The sorghum is in spike.

I walk on slowly,

My heart stupefied.

Those who know me say that my heart is sad;

Those who do not know me ask for what I am
searching.

Oh, grey heaven stretching endlessly away,

Who has done this to me?

The millet is dense and tall,

The sorghum is in grain.

I walk on slowly,

My heart like to choke.

Those who know me say that my heart is sad;

Those who do not know me ask for what I am
searching.

Oh, grey heaven stretching endlessly away,

Who has done this to me?

My Man Is on Service

MY man is on service

For how long no one knows.

Oh, when will he return?

The fowls are roosting on their perches,

Another day is done,

Down the hill come cattle and sheep;

But my man is on service

And how can I forget him?

My man is on service,

The days and months go by.

Oh, when will he be home again?

The fowls have come to their roosts,

Another day is done,

Sheep and cattle are back in the pen

But my man is on service,

Thirsty, perhaps, and hungry.

I Beg You, Zhongzi

I beg you, Zhongzi,
Don't climb into our yard,
Don't break our willows!
Not that I mind about the willows,
But I am afraid of my father and mother.
Yes, much as I love you,
I am afraid of what my parents will say.

I beg you, Zhongzi,
Don't climb over our wall,
Don't break our mulberry trees!
Not that I mind about the mulberries,
But I am afraid of my brothers.
Yes, much as I love you,
I dread what my brothers will say.

I beg you, Zhongzi,
Don't climb into our garden,
Don't break our elms!
Not that I mind about the elms,
But I am afraid folk will gossip;
Yes, much as I love you,
I am afraid of their gossip.

The Wife Says: "The Cock Is Crowing."

THE wife says: "The cock is crowing."
The husband replies: "It's hardly dawn."
"Get up and look at the night sky,
The morning star is high and bright."
"I'll get up at my ease,
And go to shoot wild ducks and geese."

"When you shoot, you'll make a good bag,
And I'll dress them well for you.
With these delicacies we'll drink
To a blissful old age.
With such harmonious love,
All will be happy and peaceful."

"Knowing your deep concern for me,
A colourful jade pendant I'll present you.
Knowing your tender feeling for me,
A colourful jade pendant I'll give you.
Knowing your virtuous love for me,
A colourful jade pendant I'll requite you."

If You Really Love Me

IF you really love me,
Lift up your robe and wade across the River Zhen!
If you don't love me,
What about some other man?
Oh, the most foolish among fools are you!

If you really love me,
Lift up your robe and wade across the River Wei!
If you don't love me,
What about someone else?
Oh, the most foolish among fools are you!

Wind and Rain

COLD is the wind and chill the rain,
Hens are cackling loudly.
Now I've seen my good man again,
How peaceful my heart is!

The wind whistles and the rain patters,
Hens are cackling merrily.
Now I've seen my good man again,
How light my heart becomes!

Wind and rain sweep the gloomy sky,
Hens are cackling endlessly.
Now I've seen my good man again,
How joyful my heart feels!

Scholar with the Blue Collar

OH, scholar with the blue collar,
Long I've been yearning for you.
Though I haven't gone to visit you,
Why don't you send me some news?

Oh, scholar with the blue silk ribbon,
Long I've been in love with you.
Though I haven't gone to visit you,
Why don't you come to see me?

I keep pacing to and fro,
On the tower of the city wall.
If for one day I don't see you,
It seems like three months to me!

Outside the Eastern City Gate

OUTSIDE the eastern city gate,
Girls look like colourful clouds.
Though they are lovely as clouds,
Yet none is the one who dwells in my heart.
Only she of the white dress and greenish scarf
Would I be eager to meet.

Outside the outer city gate,
Girls look like reed catkins.
Though they are pretty as reed catkins,
Yet none is the one who remains in my heart.
Only she of the white dress and scarlet kerchief
Would I be overjoyed to see.

In the Wilds Grew Creepers

IN the wilds grew creepers,
With dew-drops so heavy and thick.
There was a girl, beautiful and bright,
Her features so delicate and charming.
By chance we met each other,
She embodied my long-cherished wish.

In the wilds grew creepers,
With dew-drops so full and round.
There was a girl, beautiful and bright,
Her features so charming and delicate.
By chance we met each other,
Together with her life will be happy.

When the Zhen and the Wei

WHEN the Zhen and the Wei
Brim their banks,
Lads and lasses
Gather orchids.
Says she, "Have you looked around?"
Says he, "I have."
"Why not have another look?
Beyond the Wei
It's very open and pleasant."
Together then
They sport and play,
And each gives the other a peony.

When the Zhen and the Wei
Flow clear,

Lads and lasses

Flock to their banks.

Says she, "Have you looked around?"

Says he, "I have."

"Why not have another look?

Beyond the Wei

It's very open and pleasant."

Together then

They sport and play,

And each gives the other a peony.

This song describes the spring outing in the third month, a time for courtship, when young people gathered by rivers. The peony symbolized true love.

Chop, Chop, We Cut Elms

CHOP, chop, we cut down the elms

And pile the wood on the bank,

By the waters clear and rippling.

They neither sow nor reap;

How then have they three hundred sheaves of corn?

They neither hunt nor chase;

How then do we see badgers hanging in their courtyards?

Ah, those lords,

They do not need to work for their food!

Chop, chop, we cut wood for wheel-spokes

And pile it on the shore,

By the waters clear and flowing.

They neither sow nor reap;

How then have they three hundred stacks of corn?
They neither hunt nor chase;
How then do we see bulls hanging in their court-
    yards?
Ah, those lords
They do not need to work to eat!

Chop, chop, we cut hard wood for wheels
And pile it at the river's brink,
By the waters clear and dimpling.
They neither sow nor reap;
How then have they three hundred ricks of corn?
They neither hunt nor chase;
How then do we see quails hanging in their court-
    yards?
Ah, those lords
They do not have to work to live!

Field Mouse

FIELD mouse, field mouse,*
Keep away from our millet!
Three years we have served you
But what do you care about us?
Now we shall leave you
For a happier realm,
A happy realm
Where we shall have a place.

Field mouse, field mouse,
Keep away from our wheat!
Three years we have served you,
But what have you done for us?

---

* A term used to indicate the despotic ruler.

Now we shall leave you

For a happier land,

A happy land

Where we shall get our due.

Field mouse, field mouse,

Keep away from our rice-shoots!

Three years we have served you,

But have you rewarded us?

Now we shall leave you

For those happy plains,

Those happy plains

Where weeping is never heard.

Tightly Bound

TIGHTLY bound is a bundle of firewood,

The Three Stars* are high in the sky.

Oh, which night is tonight?

Here I meet my good man.

What fortune! What fortune!

How lucky to see my good man!

Tightly bound is a bundle of hay,

The Three Stars are at the corner of the house.

Oh, which night is tonight?

Here I meet my unknown spouse.

What fortune! What fortune!

How lucky to see my unknown spouse!

---

* The interpretations for this are varied, among which one explains that in the first stanza this refers to Orion's belt and the line indicates the season; in the second stanza it refers to three bright stars in Scorpio and the line indicates that it is late evening; in the third stanza it refers to Altair and the line indicates it is the middle of the night.

Tightly bound is a bundle of brambles,
The Three Stars are in front of the door.
Oh, which night is tonight?
Here I meet my beautiful one.
What fortune! What fortune!
How lucky to see my beautiful one!

Bustards' Plumes

SWISH, swish sound the bustards' plumes,
Alighting on a clump of oaks.
The king's corvée gives no peace and rest,
Impossible for me to plant millet!
What can my parents depend on for their living?
Good Heavens! Good Heavens!
When shall I lead a life of leisure?

Swish, swish flap the bustards' wings,
Alighting on a clump of brambles.
The king's corvée gives no peace and rest,
Impossible for me to plant millet!
What can my parents rely on for their support?
Good Heavens! Good Heavens!
When will all this come to an end?

Swish, swish come the row of bustards,
Alighting on a clump of mulberries.
The king's corvée gives no peace and rest,
Impossible for me to plant rice!
What can my parents depend on for their meals?
Good Heavens! Good Heavens!
When will life resume its peace?

The Reeds

THE reeds are luxuriant and green,
The white dew has turned to frost.
My beloved so dear to me
Is somewhere beyond the waters.
Upriver I search for him,
The way is arduous and long.
Downriver I search for him,
He seems to be in the middle of the waters.

The reeds are exuberant and strong,
The white dew has not yet dried.
My beloved so dear to me
Is somewhere near the river-bank.
Upriver I search for him,
The way is arduous and hard.

Downriver I search for him,

He seems to be on a shoal in the waters.

The reeds are flourishing and lush,

The white dew is still falling.

My beloved so dear to me

Is somewhere near the riverside.

Upriver I search for him,

The way is arduous and tortuous.

Downriver I search for him,

He seems to be on an islet in the waters.

The Golden Oriole Sings

THE golden oriole sings

As it lights on the thorn-bush.

Who has gone with Duke Mu to the grave?

Yanxi of the Ziju clan.

This Yanxi

Was a match for a hundred men.

When we approach the tomb

We shake with dread.

Grey heaven

Slays all our best men!

Could we but ransom him,

There are a hundred who would give their lives.

This song laments three men of the Ziju clan who were buried
live with Duke Mu of Qin after his death in 622 B.C.

The golden oriole sings
As it lights on the mulberry.
Who has gone with Duke Mu to the grave?
Zhonghang of the Ziju clan.
This Zhonghang
Could stand up to a hundred men.
When we approach the tomb
We shake with dread.
Grey heaven
Slays all our best men!
Could we but ransom him,
There are a hundred who would give their live

The golden oriole sings
As it lights on the brambles.
Who has gone with Duke Mu to the grave?
Qianhu of the Ziju clan.
This Qianhu
Could withstand a hundred men.

When we approach the tomb
We shake with dread.
Grey heaven
Slays all our best men!
Could we but ransom him,
There are a hundred who would give their lives.

How Can You Say You Have No Clothes?

HOW can you say you have no clothes?
I'll share with you my padded robe.
The king's dispatching his troops to battle,
Let's make ready our dagger-axes and spears.
Together with you, I'll fight our common foe.

How can you say you have no clothes?
I'll share with you my undershirt.
The king's dispatching his troops to battle,
Let's make ready our lances and halberds.
Together with you, I'll set off to war.

How can you say you have no clothes?
I'll share with you my humble skirt.

The king's dispatching his troops to battle,
Let's make ready our armour and weapons.
Together with you, I'll march to the front.

In the Lowlands Grows the Carambola

IN the lowlands grows the carambola,
Tender and graceful are its branches.
So sturdy and beautiful you look,
I'm happy you have no feelings.

In the lowlands grows the carambola,
Tender and graceful are its blossoms.
So sturdy and beautiful you look,
I'm happy you have no home.

In the lowlands grows the carambola,
Tender and graceful is its fruit.
So sturdy and beautiful you look,
I'm happy you have no family.

In the Seventh Month

IN the seventh month Antares sinks in the west,

In the ninth, cloth is handed out for making
clothes,

In the eleventh month the wind blows keen,

In the twelfth the weather turns cold;

But without a coat, with nothing warm to wear,

How can we get through the year?

In the first month mend the ploughs,

In the second go out to work

With wives and young ones,

Taking food to the southern fields

To please the overseer.

In the seventh month Antares sinks in the west,

In the ninth, cloth is handed out for making
clothes;

As the spring grows warm
And the oriole sings,
The girls taking deep baskets
Go along the small paths
To gather tender mulberry leaves;
As the spring days lengthen
They pluck artemisia by the armful;
But their hearts are not at ease
Lest they be carried off by the lord's son.

In the seventh month Antares sinks in the west,
In the eighth, we gather rushes,
In the third, we prune the mulberry,
Taking chopper and bill
To lop off the long branches
And bind up the tender leaves.
In the seventh month the shrike cries,
In the eighth, we twist thread,
Black and yellow;
I use a bright red dye
To colour a garment for the lord's son.

In the fourth month the milkwort is in spike,

In the fifth, the cicada cries;

In the eighth, the harvest is gathered,

In the tenth, down come the leaves;

In the eleventh we make offerings before the chase,

We hunt wild-cats and foxes

For furs for our lord.

In the twelfth month the hunters meet

And drill for war;

The smaller boars we keep,

The larger ones we offer to our lord.

In the fifth month the locust moves its legs,

In the sixth, the grasshopper shakes its wings.

In the seventh, the cricket is in the fields,

In the eighth, it moves under the eaves,

In the ninth, to the door,

And in the tenth under the bed.

We clear the corners to smoke out rats,

Paste up north windows and plaster the door with
    mud.

Come, wife and children,

The turn of the year is at hand,

Let us move inside.

In the sixth month we eat wild plums and cherries,

In the seventh we boil mallows and beans,

In the eighth we beat down dates,

In the tenth we boil rice

To brew wine for the spring,

A cordial for the old.

In the seventh month we eat melon,

In the eighth cut the gourds,

In the ninth take the seeding hemp,

Pick lettuce and cut the ailanthus for firewood,

To give our husbandmen food.

In the ninth month we repair the threshing-floor,

In the tenth we bring in the harvest,

Millet and sorghum, early and late,

Paddy and hemp, beans and wheat.
There is no rest for farm folk:
Once harvesting is done
We are sent to work in the lord's house;
By day we gather reeds for thatch,
After dusk twist rope,
Then hurry to mend the roofs,
For it is time to sow the many grains.

In the twelfth month we chisel and hew the ice,
In the first, store it away inside cold sheds,
In the second it is brought out
For the sacrifice with lambs and garlic;
In the ninth month the weather is chill,
In the tenth, we sweep and clear the threshing-
floor;
With twin pitchers we start the feast,
Killing a young lamb,
Then go up to the hall
And raise the cup of buffalo horn —
"May our lord live for ever and ever!"

Owl

OWL, oh owl!
You've taken away my fledglings,
Please don't destroy my nest.
With such love and pains,
I toiled to hatch the young ones.

Before the spell of wet weather,
I stripped some bits off the mulberry's roots
To mend my nest, window and door.
But the people down below,
Will perhaps dare to bully me.

I worked extremely hard,
Going to and fro to gather reed catkins

Which I kept storing up.
And my beak was sore and weary,
Yet still I have no house of my own.

My feathers are torn and sparse,
My tail has lost its gloss.
My nest's swaying and tottering,
At the mercy of wind and rain.
And in alarm I can't help crying.

The Eastern Hills

I was sent to the eastern hills,

Long, long was I away;

Now, as I return from the east,

A light, fine rain is falling.

On my way from the east,

My heart yearns for the west;

I shall make myself a farmer's clothing,

May I never go to wars again!

Wild silkworms twist and turn

Long days on the mulberry bush;

And I curled up to sleep alone

Beneath my cart.

I was sent to the eastern hills,

Long, long was I away;

Now, as I return from the east,

A light, fine rain is falling.

Perhaps the bryony vine

Will have clambered over my eaves,

I'll find woodlice in my room,

And cobwebs across the door,

Deer-tracks in the paddock

And the glimmer of will-o'-the-wisps.

A sorry sight —

But how I long to see it!

I was sent to the eastern hills,

Long, long was I away;

Now, as I return from the east,

A light, fine rain is falling.

A stork is crying on the mound,

My wife sighs in her cottage;

Let all the corners be sprinkled and swept,

I am coming back from the wars!

That round gourd,

Long ago left on the wood-pile,

Three years have gone by

Since last I saw it!

I was sent to the eastern hills,

Long, long was I away;

Now, as I return from the east,

A light, fine rain is falling.

When the oriole takes flight,

Its wings glint;

When my bride came to my house,

Her horses were bay and white, sorrel and white;

Her mother tied the wedding sash for her;

There was no end to the rites.

To be newly married was bliss;

How will it be, after these years, to meet again?

We Gather Vetch

WE gather vetch, gather vetch,
While the young shoots are springing;
Oh, to go back, go back;
But the year is ending.
We have no house, no home,
Because of the Huns;
We cannot sit or take rest,
Because of the Huns.

We gather vetch, gather vetch,
While the shoots are tender;
Oh, to go back, go back;
Our hearts are sad.
Our sad hearts burn,

And we hunger and thirst;

But our garrison duty drags on,

And no messenger goes to take news home.

We gather vetch, gather vetch,

But the shoots are tough;

Oh, to go back, go back;

The tenth month is here again,

But the king's business is unending;

We cannot sit or take rest;

Our sad hearts are racked with pain,

And no one comes to comfort us on our march.

What splendid blossom is that?

It is the blossom of the cherry-tree.

What great chariot is that?

It is the chariot of a nobleman.

His war-chariot stands ready yoked

With four proud stallions;

How can we settle in one place?
We march to three different posts in a month.

The four stallions are yoked
To make a sturdy team;
The noblemen ride in the chariot,
We take cover behind;
Four stately stallions,
Ivory bow-ends and a fish-skin quiver;
Every day we must be on our guard,
We are hard-pressed by the Huns.

When we left home
The willows were softly swaying;
Now as we turn back
Snowflakes fly.
Our road is a long one
And we thirst and hunger,
Our hearts are filled with sorrow;
But who knows our misery?

Silks, Oh So Bright

SILKS, oh so bright,

Make up this shell-embroidery.

Those slanderers

Have really gone too far!

Their mouths, agape,

Make up the Southern Fan.*

Those slanderers —

Who are their counsellors?

Whispering gossip,

They plot to slander men.

Be careful what you say!

The day will come when nobody believes you.

---

* The Southern Fan was another name for the Winnowing Fan,
a constellation in the sky.

With ready tongues
They plot to make up lies.
Though some are taken in,
One day they will turn against you.

The proud are gloating,
Toilers' hearts are sad.
Ah, Heaven, grey Heaven,
Take note of those proud men,
Have pity on the toilers.

Those slanderers —
Who are their counsellors?
Let us seize those rumour-mongers
And throw them to wolves and tigers!
If no wolves or tigers will eat them,
Let us send them to the Far North;
If the Far North will not accept them,
Let us give them to Old Man Heaven.

The road to Willow Garden
Is by Mu Hill;
There lives the eunuch Mengzi
Who made this song.
May all gentlemen, whosoever they be,
Listen to it with attention!

The Eastern States*

VESSELS are brimming with food,

And spoons have long, curved handles;

Smooth as a grindstone is the royal road

And straight as an arrow;

Noblemen walk on that road;

Humble folk can only look at it;

Longingly I turn to gaze at it;

My tears flow in a flood.

In the eastern states far and near,

Shuttles and spools are bare.

Wearing close-woven slippers

Which keep out the winter frost,

---

*Contrasting his life with that of the people of Zhou, a man of the subordinate eastern states criticizes the central Zhou government. He refers to stars which do not live up to their names, to show the falsity and absurdity of the times.

The handsome sons of nobles
Stride down the royal highway;
They pass to and fro,
And the sight sickens me.

Cold water flowing from springs,
Do not soak our firewood!
I sigh bitterly,
Worn out and wretched.
Fuel for the stove
Can be carted away,
But for me, worn out and wretched,
Is there no rest?

The men of the east
Toil hard and get no comfort,
While the men of the west
Are splendidly arrayed;

The sons of their boatmen
Wear bearskins,
The sons of retainers
Serve as officials.

Some men have wine,
Others not even the lees;
Some men have round jade pendants,
Others not even the strings.
In heaven there is a Milky Way,
A mirror which can only shine;
There the Weaving Maid, her legs astride
Moves seven times in one day.

But though seven times she moves,
Not one pattern does she weave.
Bright shines the Ox,
But it cannot be yoked to a cart;

In the east is the Morning Star,
And the Evening Star in the west,
The net with the curved handle in the sky
Is set on a public highway.

In the south there is a Winnowing Fan,
But it cannot be used to sift grain;
In the north there is a Dipper,
But it cannot ladle wine.
The Winnowing Fan in the south
Only sucks its tongue;
The Dipper in the north
Has a high handle pointing west.

he Northern Hills

I climb the northern hills
Picking the boxthorn.
Zealous officials
Must labour day and night;
The king's business is endless,
Causing our parents worry for their sons.

Everywhere under the sky
Is the king's dominion;
To the uttermost ends of the earth
All men are his servants;
But the tasks are unequal
And I have more work than the rest.

A team of four gallops on and on,
The king's business is unending;
I am congratulated on my youth,
Complimented on my vigour;
While my muscles are strong
I have business on every hand.

Some men rest idle at home,
Others wear themselves out in the service of the
    state;
Some lie quiet in bed,
Others are always on the move;

Some have never heard weeping or wailing,
Others toil without rest;
Some loll at ease,
Others are harassed working for the king;

Some take pleasure in wine,

Others have no respite from care;

Some just go round airing their views,

Others are left with all the work.

In the Beginning Who Gave Birth to Our People?

IN the beginning who gave birth to our people?

It was Jiang Yuan.

How did she give birth to our people?

By earnest sacrifice and prayer

That she might no longer be childless.

She trod on God's big toe print,

Standing alone at rest there;

She conceived, lived quietly,

Then gave birth and nursed the child,

And he was Hou Ji.*

---

* The name Hou Ji in the legend means Prince Millet.

When she had fulfilled her months,

Her first-born came like a lamb,

With no bursting or rending,

With no hurt or harm,

To manifest power divine.

But she feared that God was displeased

And had not blessed her sacrifice and prayer,

That the child had been born in vain!

So she abandoned him in a narrow lane,

But oxen and sheep protected and nurtured him;

Then she abandoned him in a great forest,

But it chanced that woodcutters came to this forest;

Then she abandoned him on the cold ice,

But birds covered him with their wings;

When the birds flew off,

Hou Ji began to wail.

So long he wailed and loud,

His voice was heard on the road.

Then the child began to crawl,
Rose to his feet and learned
To seek food with his mouth.
He planted beans,
The beans grew sturdy and tall;
His millet flourished,
His hemp and wheat grew thick,
His young gourds teemed.

Indeed, Hou Ji knew the way
To make crops grow well.
He cleared away the rank weeds,
He sowed good yellow grain,
It grew straight and sturdy,
It was heavy and tall;
It sprouted and eared;
It grew firm and good,
Thick and full.
Then he made his home in Tai.

Thus it was that the lucky grain came down,

The black millet, the double-kernelled,

The red millet and the white.

Far and wide the black millet and the double-
kernelled

Field after field he reaped;

Far and wide the red millet and the white

He carried in his arms, bore on his back,

And brought home for the sacrifice.

What are they, our sacrifices?

We hull the grain and ladle it from the mortar,

Sift it, soften it by treading,

Swill and scour it,

Then steam it thoroughly.

Next, taking careful thought,

We pluck artemisia, make offering of fat,

Skin a ram,

Then roast and broil it,

To bring a good harvest in the coming year.

We heap the offerings on wooden stands,

On wooden stands, in earthenware vessels;

When the fragrance rises up,

God on high is well pleased:

What smell is this, so good and strong?

Hou Ji founded this sacrifice

To propitiate the gods,

And it has come down to this day.

China's Earliest Anthology of Poetry

Yu Guanying

THE *Book of Songs* is the earliest anthology of poetry in China. The three hundred and five songs in this collection date from between the eleventh and the sixth century B.C. and were probably compiled into one book in the sixth century B.C. According to the *Zuo Zhuan*,* when Lord Ji Zha of Wu went to the state of Lu in 544 B.C. to hear its music, the ancient songs sung for him were arranged in the same order with similar titles for the different categories as in the *Book of Songs* which we have today. In the year 544 B.C., Confucius was only eight years old, and later he too referred to this collection as the *Three Hundred Songs*. From this it is clear that in the time of Confucius there was already an anthology known as the *Three Hundred Songs* which was much the same as our present *Book of Songs*. Some later scholars claimed that the *Book of Songs* was com-

Yu Guanying, a research fellow in the Institute of Chinese Literature of the Chinese Academy of Social Sciences, has made a special study of the *Book of Songs* and the *yuefu* songs dating from the second century B.C. to the sixth century A.D. His publications include *Essays on the Poetry of the Six Dynasties*.

* Annals written at the beginning of the Warring States Period recording events between 722 and 468 B.C.

piled by Confucius himself, and that he cut out certai
songs; but there is little ground for this claim.

Since all the songs in this anthology were set to m
sic and kept by the royal musicians of the House
Zhou, it is likely that the earliest compiler of the colle
tion was a professional musician. The book is divide
according to the type of music into four main section
guofeng xiaoya, daya and *song*. The *guofeng*, c
songs of the city states which were fiefs of the House
Zhou, include folk-songs from fifteen different localitie
The *ya* are set to another type of music; and with fe
exceptions both the *xiaoya* (lesser *ya*) and the *day*
(greater *ya*) were composed during the Western Zh
period between the eleventh and the eighth century B.
and came from the vicinity of Western Zhou. There
no satisfactory and reliable explanation for the diffe
ence between the *xiaoya* and *daya*. Possibly the
was one form of ceremonial or festive music, and wh
a newer type influenced by folk-songs came into fashi
the earlier variety was called *daya* and the newer *xia*
ya. The *song* are songs of praise or hymns used duri
sacrifices, and this section is subdivided into the Hym
of Zhou, the Hymns of Shang and the Hymns of L
of which the Hymns of Zhou are the oldest, dating fro
between the eleventh and the ninth century B.C. duri
the early part of the Zhou Dynasty. The Hymns
Shang from the state of Song, founded by the desce
dants of the House of Shang, were written in the eigh
and seventh centuries B.C. The Hymns of Lu we
composed in the state of Lu in the seventh century B.

Most of the *guofeng* songs and some of the *xiao*
are folk-songs; and these make up the most importa
part of the anthology. The early records do not tell

ow these folk-songs came to be collected and kept by
ne royal musicians of the Zhou court, and we may sur-
ise that they were first gathered together by the min-
rels of the vassal states, who looked for folk-songs to
nrich their repertoire. Then the music of the vassal
ates was presented to the Zhou overlord and kept by
ne royal house. Some scholars of the Han Dynasty
206 B.C.-A.D. 220) claimed that during the Zhou
Dynasty certain officials travelled the country to collect
ongs and present them to the royal musicians. Others
aid that the government paid old musicians who had no
amilies to go and seek out for the royal court the songs
f the various states. These later accounts differ be-
ause they were simply conjecture.

A number of the songs were composed by members
f the ruling class. Probably most of the hymns and
oems embodying advice to the ruler were written by
fficials to present to the Zhou court, while the songs
sed in ancestral sacrifices and the feasts given to guests,
r before going to war and hunting, were composed by
fficial diviners and historians. Other songs were made
y minor officials, not at the order of the government
r to be presented at court but to express personal indignation; and these were very likely collected with
olk-songs by the royal musicians.

The official musicians were the first to teach these
ongs, for songs and music formed the major part of the
ducation of young nobles in the Zhou Dynasty. By the
ime of Confucius in the sixth century B.C., education
was in the hands of private tutors, but the songs were
till the main part of their teaching. The Zhou-dynasty
nobles put songs to a practical purpose, using them
during ceremonies and to offer advice on state policy,

while in daily life they added distinction to a man'
conversation and helped to express his feelings. Youn
lovers used them to tell their love, and through them
envoys were often able to convey their ideas diplomat
ically. Confucius attached so much importance to th
study of the old songs that he said, "A man who doe
not study the songs cannot speak." Later Confucian
also studied the *Three Hundred Songs* and had them
set to music, quoting from them frequently in discussion
on philosophy. Thus the study of the songs persisted
amongst Confucians during the Warring States Perioc
down to the third century B.C. and the *Three Hundrec
Songs* became one of the classical canons of Confu
cianism.

Positive chronology is out of the question for mos
poems in the *Book of Songs*, although approximat
dates may be given for some. By and large, they can be
attributed to three periods: the early part of the West
ern Zhou Dynasty from the eleventh to the ninth century
B.C., the later part of the Western Zhou Dynasty dur
ing the ninth and the eighth century B.C., and the
Eastern Zhou Dynasty from the eighth to the sixth
century B.C. They reflect many aspects of the life o
those periods.

Songs of the early Western Zhou period include
all the Hymns of Zhou, a small part of the *daya* and
a few of the *guofeng*. The majority of these are narra
tive or historical poems, the most outstanding being
"In the Beginning Who Gave Birth to Our People?'
"Stalwart Was Liu the Duke" and "The Young Gourd
Spread and Spread", which describe in verse the found
ing of the Zhou Dynasty.

"In the Beginning Who Gave Birth to Our People?" tells the story of Hou Ji, the legendary ancestor of the Zhou people and reputedly the first farmer. Hou Ji's mother Jiang Yuan conceived him after treading on the footprint of a god, but she dared not keep the child. This verse describes how Hou Ji was abandoned:

> So she abandoned him in a narrow lane,
> But oxen and sheep protected and nurtured him;
> Then she abandoned him in a great forest,
> But it chanced that woodcutters came to this
>   forest;
> Then she abandoned him on the cold ice,
> But birds covered him with their wings;
> When the birds flew off,
> Hou Ji began to wail.
> So long he wailed and loud,
> His voice was heard on the road.

This shows vividly and concisely Hou Ji's uniqueness from birth and the divine protection he enjoyed. More wonderful still, as soon as he grew up he knew how to plough and grow grain, and the song describes the abundance of his various crops; for this hero personifies the determination of the men of old to conquer nature, their inventiveness and ingenuity. Songs like this were obviously based on early legends, handed down by word of mouth.

"Stalwart Was Liu the Duke" relates how this ancestor of the Zhous, Duke Liu, led his people from Tai to Bin, where they opened up wasteland, built houses and settled down. "The Young Gourds Spread and Spread" describes a descendant of Duke Liu named

Tanfu, who migrated from Bin to Mount Qi. First he
and his companions lived in caves, then they tilled the
land, erected an ancestral temple, trained an army and
defeated their enemies. These two songs are not full
of miraculous happenings like the first but describe the
two great migrations in a plain and matter-of-fact way,
giving forceful expression to the people's joy in pioneer-
ing and their industry.

Songs describing agriculture are important material
for our study of early Zhou society. The best of this
kind among the Hymns of Zhou are "They Clear Away
the Grass, the Trees" and "Very Sharp, the Good
Shares" and "In the Seventh Month" from the *guofeng*.
The last, which we are presenting to readers here, describes the serfs' life and feelings throughout the year,
and the countryside they lived in. Each family has to
work hard and is heavily exploited. They plough, weave,
hunt, build houses, store ice and brew wine for their
master, but go hungry themselves and complain:

> But without a coat, with nothing warm to wear,
> How can we get through the year?

But hunger and cold are not all they have to contend
with, as we see from the second stanza:

> As the spring grows warm
> And the oriole sings,
> The girls taking deep baskets
> Go along the small paths
> To gather tender mulberry leaves;
> As the spring days lengthen
> They pluck artemisia by the armful;

But their hearts are not at ease
Lest they be carried off by the lord's son.

Some poems of this period take war as their theme and voice the people's hatred of fighting. Thus "The Eastern Hills", included in our selection, was probably written by a soldier on his way home from a campaign. On the road he looks forward to reaching home and living as an ordinary citizen again; in imagination he sees his house sadly neglected, his wife longing for him far away; and he believes their reunion will be even happier than their wedding day. This poem with its stirring expression of men's longing for a peaceful life is a fine, compelling folk-song.

From this brief account we can see that narrative poetry predominates in the songs of this period; but there are a few lyrics too in the *guofeng* which are more skilfully written than the hymns and court odes.

The songs of the later Western Zhou period include most of the *daya* and practically all the *xiaoya*, as well as a few from the *guofeng*. The best poems of this age are some of the *xiaoya*, quite a few of which are folk-songs.

The middle of the ninth century B.C. and the first part of the eighth were times of bad rule in Chinese history when the country was raided many times by northern tribesmen; hence a number of the songs of these periods express popular discontent and dissatisfaction with the government. One poem in the *daya* tells how whole families were driven from their homes to perish, while the survivors were like the dying embers of a fire and the state was tottering to its ruin. Another poem attacks the rulers for wilfully neglecting their duties in order to carouse and amuse themselves. Both these attacks on the royal house were written by nobles. An example we have chosen of songs on social injustice is "The Northern Hills", which points out that some officials led a life of leisure while others did all the hard work.

> Some men rest idle at home,
> Others wear themselves out in the service of the
>   state;
> Some lie quiet in bed,
> Others are always on the move;
>
> Some have never heard weeping or wailing,
> Others toil without rest;
> Some loll at ease,
> Others are harassed working for the king;
>
> Some take pleasure in wine,
> Others have no respite from care;
> Some just go round airing their views,
> Others are left with all the work.

This penetrating contrast between minor officials and the great shows the sharp difference between the higher and the lower ranks at court; and though the writer was expressing his personal resentment, he reveals a general inequality.

Another song in our selection, "The Eastern States" voices the hatred of the conquered people of the east for the Zhous, describing how as a result of pillage and exploitation by the Western Zhou conquerors even "shuttles and spools are bare", and contrasting the easy life of the Zhous with the misery of the men of the eastern states. The poet enumerates the stars in heaven which do not live up to their fine names: the Winnowing Fan cannot winnow, the Dipper cannot hold wine and its handle is turned towards the west so that the Zhous can use it to plunder the east. These strange images vent the poet's indignation by showing that there is deceit even in the sky — even Heaven is unjust. This is a remarkable song with its depth of feeling and unusual artistic technique.

If these personal laments and satirical poems reflect the serious social contradictions of that time, there are odes in the *daya* and *xiaoya* which extol the military prowess of King Xuan of Zhou, who reigned at the end of the ninth and the beginning of the eighth century B.C. and who led expeditions against the frontier tribes. One song describes his attack on the Xu tribes in the east, another his northern expedition against the Huns, yet another his campaign against the Jing tribes in the south. These spirited, vigorous yet dignified odes were written by officials or historians. But although competent enough, they cannot compare with soldiers' songs like "We Gather Vetch" in the *xiaoya*.

"We Gather Vetch" also dates from the reign of King Xuan and tells of the hardships of the garrison troops stationed at the distant frontiers to keep back the Huns. The last verse gives a moving and very human description of a soldier's misery when, bound home at last, he suffers from cold and hunger on the road.

> When we left home
> The willows were softly swaying;
> Now as we turn back

Snowflakes fly.
Our road is a long one
And we thirst and hunger,
Our hearts are filled with sorrow;
But who knows our misery?

Another song of this period, "What Grass Would Not Turn Yellow?" voices conscripts' dissatisfaction at being sent out to the four borders of the land, far from their wives. The poet laments, "Alas for the soldiers treated as less than men!" Protests and accusations of this kind contrast sharply with the poems praising the king's might.

The bulk of the songs of this period are in the *xiaoya*, and quite a number of them are satires or lamentations which reflect a large variety of social contradictions. Although not a few deal with the life of nobles, the tone is different from that in the *daya*, and there are lyrics too which are akin to folk-songs.

All the songs of the Eastern Zhou Dynasty, apart from the Hymns of Shang and the Hymns of Lu, come from the *guofeng*. Since the majority are folk-songs, in them we can hear the authentic voices of those who were hungry and knew no rest, while a number reflect the struggle between rulers and ruled more clearly than the songs of the preceding period. "Chop, Chop, We Cut Elms" and "Field Mouse" are examples of this. The former points out that although the nobles neither plough nor hunt, their storehouses are full of grain while game hangs in their courtyards; and the poet asks sarcastically how they are able to eat without working. The second poem compares the exploiter to a field mouse, aptly exposing the true nature of the exploiting class. The longing to go to "a happy land", in other words a society free from tyranny and exploitation, was of course an empty dream at that time; yet it shows the author's rebellious spirit.

Many of the *guofeng* protest against the oppressive system of corvée and conscription. "Bastards' Plumes" is a heartfelt denunciation of this type. When the peasants were conscripted, their fields lay waste and their parents had nothing to eat; yet they never knew how long the term of service would last. They could only complain and call upon heaven in their wretchedness.

Attacks on the rulers' despotism and disgraceful behaviour in the *guofeng* are sometimes more scathing than those in the earlier songs. For instance, "There Is a Thorny Date-tree at the Tomb Gate" condemns a tyrant bluntly described as "no good". The poet's decision to cut down the tree with his axe shows his desire to do away with this ruler.

Songs about love and marriage form the bulk of the *guofeng*, and most of these are folk-songs; but though their theme is the same they possess great variety, presenting all the sadness and joy of lovers' partings and reunions. Many descriptions of first encounters, pledges of faith and secret assignations show the relative freedom of love in those days for ordinary people and the primitive social conditions. "The Roebuck" tells how a hunter in the woods meets a girl whom he finds as lovely as jade, and how he wins her. The fresh openness of feeling here harmonizes with the sense of spring in the countryside. "The Quiet Girl", another song in our selection, relates how two lovers arrange to meet at the city wall; but when the young man comes the girl hides herself, throwing him into an anxious quandary. The ingenuous couple in this poem are full of life. Other songs which describe young people singing and dancing or young lovers meeting during festivals are pulsing with joy and reveal a comparative freedom in love. But that certain restrictions existed can be seen from songs like "I Beg You, Zhongzi" included in our selection, in which a girl longs for her lover but dares not let him come to her because she dreads what her parents, her brothers and the neighbours will say. In "Sailing a Barge of Cypress" a mother interferes with her daughter's marriage, but the girl resists and boldly declares that her love will never change until she dies. She protests bitterly at the obstacles put in her way, crying: "Ah, mother! Ah, heaven! What makes you so cruel and hard?"

"A Gust of Wind from the Valley" and one of the songs in our selection, "A Simple Fellow", are ballads about wives forsaken by their husbands. The weak, good woman in the first song complains that her husband is interested in someone else and has tired of his old wife, and she reminds him of their former love. But the woman in the second poem is a stronger character, who expresses more regret than sorrow and is eager to break with her husband because she has no feeling left for him. Bitter experience has taught her that even in love there is no equality between the sexes. Of the two poems, this is the more moving because it goes deeper into the woman's feelings and state of mind.

Some of the *guofeng* describe various tasks, as in "In the Seventh Month", which gives a fairly comprehensive picture of the work of the peasants. These songs were often composed at work or to accompany it. Thus another song in our selection "Gathering Plantain" was sung by girls plucking this herb. The three stanzas, twelve lines in all, repeat each other except for the use of six different verbs to show the whole process from setting out to returning with full skirts; and the simple words and rhythm are gay and evocative. In "Fibreshoes Closely Fastened" a woman slave is making clothes for her mistress, who turns away scornfully when they are offered to her and ignores the slave. Thus the poem ends: "So small-minded is she, I have made this song to show her up." This song, then unlike the others, is a deliberate satire to express a spirit of revolt.

The variety of themes is very great, as we can see from "The Golden Oriole Sings", a dirge for three good men. When Duke Mu of Qin died, many people were buried alive with him, and here the poet expresses keen regret over the death of three noblemen among them. This was actually a protest against tyranny and the barbarous custom of burying the living with the dead, a custom which had largely died out in China during the Eastern Zhou Dynasty, but appears to have persisted in the state of Qin.

Not all the *guofeng* are the work of the labouring people; some were composed by nobles. A case in point is "I Ride, I Gallop", a poem in our selection significant for its patriotic feeling. In 660 B.C., when the state of Wei was overthrown by the northern Di tribesmen, the people of Wei fled east across the Yellow River to regroup themselves in Cao, where they set up their new ruler Duke Dai of Wei. The duke's younger sister, the wife of Duke Mu of Xu, went to Cao to express her sympathy and urge that help be sought from some powerful state. When the rulers of Xu tried to stop her, she was so indignant that she wrote this song setting down her thoughts and swearing to persevere with her plan to the end. Most of the songs are anonymous; Lady Mu is the only writer who has left us a clear picture of herself in this spirited poem.

We have seen that the *Book of Songs* comprises folk-songs as well as songs by nobles, lyrics as well as narrative poems. It is clear, however, that the best part of the collection is embodied in the *guofeng* and *xiaoya*, in those songs where the people themselves sing of their lives and views on society, presenting us with a picture of their hardships and joys, what they loved and what they hated, the injuries and humiliations they suffered, and their revolt and struggle. These lovely songs are simple yet profound, reflecting the people's simple life and honest feelings. They have a universal quality, yet at the same time an individual freshness.

These songs show different aspects of the real life of that time and the outlook of different classes, and this is an important characteristic of the *Book of Songs*. Many of the poems deal with the political situation and criticize the existing society, while some made by men and women in the lowest walks of life who rebelled against exploitation and oppression reveal the basic social contradictions of that period. This realism was highly appraised by later generations and came to exercise a great influence on Chinese poets through the ages. The *yuefu* folk-songs of the Han Dynasty carried on this tradition and enlarged its influence. When poets of later centuries opposed formalistic trends in poetry, they quoted from the *Book of Songs*; and notable results were achieved in this way by Chen Zi'ang, Li

Bai and Bai Juyi in the Tang Dynasty (A.D. 618-907).

Two devices commonly employed in the *Book of Songs*, the frequent use of simile and metaphor and the practice of starting a song by evoking images quite apart from the central subject, also had a considerable influence on later writers. "Field Mouse" is a good example of a poem in which an animal is compared to a certain type of man. Sometimes the images first mentioned are related to the general theme like this, but again there may be no connection. Certain images have emotional associations; others are chosen solely for the sake of rhyme. This technique so widely used in the *guofeng* and the *xiaoya* is a distinctive rhetorical device in the *Book of Songs* and one to be found in many subsequent folk-songs, while sometimes poets borrowed the same device.

Another striking feature of these songs is the repetition of whole phrases and stanzas, done perhaps to show the development of some action, or simply for effect. Occasionally a few words of the first verse are altered to introduce a new rhyme or produce a more melodious effect. The form of repetition varies: sometimes certain stanzas are repeated, sometimes a few lines only, sometimes whole lines and phrases as in "Gathering Plantain".

The metres of Chinese classical poetry may be roughly divided into tetrasyllabic, pentasyllabic and heptasyllabic lines as well as lines of irregular length. The tetrasyllabic lines were the earliest, and most poems in the *Book of Songs* are in this form, which had already reached maturity. Those four-character lines have only two feet each; hence the rhythm is brisk compared with the five and seven-character lines which won popularity later. The great majority of the poems in the *Book of Songs* are rhymed; but the rhyme schemes show a rich variety. Rhymes may be at the end of every line or every alternate line; certain stanzas retain the same rhyme throughout; elsewhere rhymes come in the middle of a line, and sometimes they are reinforced by alliteration. The more than seventy different rhyme patterns in this anthology show how freely rhymes were used.

The vocabulary of the *Book of Songs* is a rich one; so, notably, is the use of epithets, double-adjectives, rhyming words and alliteration, which are used in a variety of ways to heighten the descriptive effect or musical quality of the songs. In addition there are choruses too and refrains, another characteristic feature of folk-poetry.

The songs in this old anthology testify to the great creative skill of the people and show clearly that attention should be paid to the study of folk-songs. Many Chinese poets in past ages were inspired by this anthology to learn from folk-poetry, and in this way new blood was infused into Chinese poetry, enabling it to develop continuously. The *Book of Songs*, which marks the glorious beginning of Chinese literature and is the fountain-head of its realist tradition, occupies a very important position in the history of Chinese literature.